ADHD for Kids, Teens and Adults

The Pathway to Your kids Success in School and Life

Laura Barkley Pinsky

Table of Contents

Introduction

Life with a kid with ADHD can be frustrating and overwhelming, but as a mother or father, there's a lot you can certainly do to help control symptoms, overcome daily problems, and bring greater calm to your loved ones.

What if you could work with your child, motivating and engage your kids in the process, to create positive change once and for all?

ADHD is a neurological disorder that triggers a variety of behavioral problems such as difficulty going to classes, concentrating on school work, maintaining projects, following instructions, completing tasks and social conversation. Once you understand how to cope, manage people with ADHD effectively, You will immensely improve their health status.

It could be challenging to differentiate between ADHD and normal child behaviour. If you spot only a few symptoms, or the symptoms appear only in a few situations, it's most likely not ADHD alternatively, if your son or daughter shows lots of ADHD signs or symptoms that can be found across all situations-at home, at college, with play-it's time for you to take a nearer look.

This book is to help kids reframe the way they think about their ADHD issue, and discover that they have special talents that are unique to them. With fun activities that engage their busy minds, This book offers parents, teachers a better understanding of kids with ADHD, their ADHD, and the simple things they can do to feel more confident and in control.

Chapter 1

ADHD In Children

Do you take into account your son or daughter may have ADHD? Here's how exactly to identify the indicators and symptoms-and get the assistance you will need.

What's ADHD or ADD?

It's normal for children to occasionally forget their research, daydream during course, work without thinking, or get fidgety in the dining area table. However, inattention, impulsivity, and hyperactivity will also be indications of Attention Deficit Hyperactivity Disorder (ADHD), sometimes referred to as Attention Deficit Disorder or ADD.

ADHD is a common neurodevelopmental disorder that typically appears early in the child years, usually prior to the generation of seven. ADHD helps it become difficult for children to inhibit their spontaneous responses-responses that may range between motion to conversation to attentiveness. Everyone knows kids who can't sit back nonetheless, who never may actually give consideration, who don't follow instructions regardless of how you present them, or who blurt out improper comments at unacceptable times. Sometimes these children are called troublemakers, or criticized to become sluggish and undisciplined. However, they could have ADHD.

CAN IT BE NORMAL CHILD BEHAVIOR, OR CAN IT BE ADHD?

Maybe it's challenging to differentiate between ADHD and normal "child behaviour." In the event that you spot just a few symptoms, or the symptoms appear only in a few situations, it's not likely ADHD alternatively, if your kid shows plenty of ADHD indicators that may be found across all situations-at home, at college, with play-it's time and energy to have a nearer look.

Life with a youngster with ADHD could be

frustrating and overwhelming, but like a father or mother, there's a whole lot you are able to do to greatly help control symptoms, overcome daily problems, and bring greater calm to all your family members.

Myths & Facts about Attention Deficit Disorder

Myth: All kids with ADHD are hyperactive

• Truth: Some children with ADHD are hyperactive, but numerous others with attention problems aren't. Children with ADHD who are inattentive, however, not excessively active, can occur to become spacey and unmotivated.

Myth: Kids with ADHD can't even give consideration.

• Fact: Children with ADHD have a tendency to have the ability to focus on actions they enjoy.

However, regardless of how hard they try, they have trouble preserving focus when the work is usually boring or repetitive.

Myth: Kids with ADHD could behave better if indeed they wished to

• Truth: Children with ADHD can do their finest to become useful, but battle to sit still, stay peaceful, or be aware. They might arrive disobedient, but that doesn't mean they're performing from purpose.

Myth: Kids will eventually grow out of ADHD

• Actuality: ADHD often continues into adulthood, so don't await your kid to outgrow the problem. Treatment might help your kid work out how to manage and minimize the symptoms.

Myth: Medication may be the best treatment option for ADHD.

• Truth: Medication is often recommended for

attention deficit disorder, nonetheless it could not end up being your very best option for your kid. Effective treatment for ADHD also includes education, behaviour therapy, support in the home and college, exercise, and proper nourishment.

JUST WHAT DOES ADHD LOOK LIKE?

When many people think about attention deficit disorder, they picture an out-of-control kid in continuous motion, bouncing from your walls and disrupting everyone around. However, the truth is far more complicated. Some children with ADHD are hyperactive, although some sit back quietly-with their attention kilometres away. Some put an excessive amount of concentration on an activity and possess trouble moving it to some other thing. Others are simply mildly inattentive, but excessively impulsive.

WHICH OF THE KIDS MAY HAVE ADHD?

- The hyperactive boy who talks nonstop and can't sit however.

- The quiet dreamer who sits at her desk and stares off into space.

- Both.

The proper answer is "C."

The indicators a youngster with Attention Deficit Disorder has, based on which characteristics predominate.

Children with ADHD could be:

• Inattentive, however, not hyperactive or impulsive.

• Hyperactive and impulsive, however in a posture to give consideration.

• Inattentive, hyperactive, and impulsive (the most frequent type of ADHD).

• Children who've inattentive symptoms of ADHD have a tendency to end up being overlooked since they're not disruptive. However, the symptoms of inattention have outcomes: obtaining back in tepid to warm water with parents and instructors for not pursuing directions; underperforming in college or clashing with other kids over not playing by the rules.

Spotting ADHD at different Ages

Because we expect very young children to become easily distractible and hyperactive, it's the impulsive behaviors-the dangerous climb; the blurted insult-that often stand out in preschoolers with ADHD. Within generation four or five 5, though, most children can see how to concentrate on others, to sit back silently when instructed to, instead of to say whatever pops with their mind. So, after plenty of time, when children reach the college-age group, some people that have ADHD stand out atlanta divorce attorneys three manners: inattentiveness, hyperactivity, and impulsivity.

Inattentiveness Indicators Of ADHD

Son daydreaming in course

It isn't that children with ADHD can't give considerations: when they're doing things they enjoy or hearing about topics where they're interested, they don't have any trouble centering and staying face to face. However, when the work is definitely recurring or tiresome, they quickly tune out.

Staying on the right course is another common problem. Children with ADHD often jump from job to job without completing a few of them or skip the necessary steps in methods. Kids with ADHD likewise have trouble focusing if things are happening around them; they often times need a quiet environment to have the ability to stay concentrated.

Symptoms of inattention in children:

- Offers trouble staying focused; is easily sidetracked or gets bored with a task before it's completed.

- Appears to never hear when spoken to

- Provides difficulty in remembering things and subsequent instructions; doesn't concentrate on details or makes careless mistakes.

- Offers trouble staying organized, preparing beforehand, and finishing projects.

- Frequently loses or misplaces homework, books, toys, or other items.

Hyperactivity Indicators Of ADHD

Probably the most apparent sign of ADHD is hyperactivity. Despite the fact that many children tend to be quite energetic, kids with hyperactive symptoms of attention deficit disorder are always moving. They will make an effort to accomplish several things simultaneously, jumping around in a single activity to some other. Even though pressured to sit back non-etheless, which might be very hard to them, their feet are tapping, their lower leg is shaking, or their fingertips are drumming.

Symptoms of hyperactivity in children:

- Constantly fidgets and squirms.

- Provides difficulty sitting still, working quietly, or relaxing.

- Checks out around regularly; often work or

climb inappropriately.

- Discussions excessively.

- May have an instantaneous temper or "brief fuse."

Impulsive Indicators Of ADHD

The impulsivity of children with ADHD could cause problems with self-control. Because they censor themselves less than additional kids do, they'll interrupt discussions, invade other people's space, ask irrelevant questions in course, make tactless observations, and also have excessively personal questions. Instructions like, "Show patience" and "Just wait a period" are sort of hard for children with ADHD to look at because they're for various other children.

Children with impulsive indicators of ADHD also have a tendency to end up being moody and to overreact emotionally. As a result of this, others can start to start to see the kid as disrespectful, odd, or needy.

Symptoms Of Impulsivity In Children:

• Functions without thinking.

• Guesses, instead of taking period to solve a problem or blurts out answers in course without ready to become called on or hear the entire question.

• Intrudes on additional people's interactions or games.

• Often interrupts others; says the wrong thing at the incorrect time.

• Failure to keep powerful feelings in balance, leading to furious outbursts or temper tantrums

Results of ADHD in children

• Boys

ADHD has nothing to do with intelligence or skill. What's more, kids with attention deficit disorder often demonstrate another positive characteristics:

•   Creativity - Children who've ADHD could be marvelously creative and imaginative. A child who daydreams and offers ten different thoughts simultaneously could become a grasp problem-solver, a fountain of ideas, or an inventive designer. Children with ADHD could be very easily sidetracked, but sometimes they notice what others don't see.

•   Versatility - Because children with ADHD take a look at many choices simultaneously, they don't become collective using one chance in the first stages and so are more open to different ideas.

•   Excitement and Spontaneity - Children with ADHD are rarely dull! They're considering a lot of varied things and also have energetic personalities. The bottom line is, if they're not exasperating you (or even though they might be), they're a lot of fun to become with.

•   Vigour and Drive - When kids with ADHD

are motivated, they work or play hard and try to succeed. It actually could be difficult to distract them from a task which makes them passionate, mainly if the knowledge is usually interactive or hands-on.

Can It Be ADHD?

A kid has symptoms of inattention, impulsivity, or hyperactivity won't mean that they has ADHD. Specific medical ailments, emotional disorders, and stressful life occasions could cause symptoms that seem to be ADHD. Before an accurate diagnosis of ADHD could be produced, you need to go to a mental doctor to explore and get rid of the pursuing options:

• Learning disabilities or problems with reading, writing, engine skills, or vocabulary.

• Major life events or distressing encounters (e.g., a recently available move, lack of life of someone you value, bullying, divorce).

• Psychological disorders, including anxiety, depression, and bipolar disorder.

• Behavioural disorders such as for example conduct disorder, reactive attachment disorder, and oppositional defiant disorder.

• Medical ailments, including thyroid problems, neurological conditions, epilepsy, and sleep issues.

Helping A Youngster With ADHD

In case your child's symptoms of inattention, hyperactivity, and impulsivity are credited to ADHD, they are able to cause many problems if remaining untreated. Children who can't concentrate and control themselves may struggle in college, enter regular trouble, and discover it hard to become friends with others or socialize. These frustrations and issues can lead to low self-esteem aswell as friction and stress for your loved ones.

However, treatment could make a dramatic difference within your child's symptoms. Using the proper support, your kid can get to become monitored for success atlanta divorce attorneys area of life. If your kid challenges with symptoms that look like ADHD, don't wait to get specialized help. You are able to treat your child's symptoms of hyperactivity, inattention, and impulsivity without diagnosis of attention deficit disorder. Options in the first place include: obtaining the child into therapy, applying an improved diet and exercise plan, and changing the home environment to lessen distractions.

In the event that you do get yourself a diagnosis of ADHD, from then on, you should use your child's doctor, therapist, and college to make a personalized treatment plan that meets his or her specific needs. Effective treatment for youth ADHD entails behavioural therapy, father or mother education and training, friendly support, and assistance at college. Medication may be used; however, it'll never be really the only attention deficit disorder treatment.

Parenting Options For Children With ADHD

"Mother, if your kid is hyperactive, inattentive, or impulsive, it could take significant amounts of vigour to get them to listen, closing a task, or sit still. The continuous monitoring could be annoying and exhausting. Sometimes you may feel like your kid is usually operating the show. However, you will find actions you may take to regain control of the problem, while simultaneously assisting your kid makes nearly all his or her abilities.

Attention Deficit Disorder isn't triggered by bad parenting, but Children with ADHD need a framework, regularity, clear communication, and rewards and implications with regards to behaviour. Besides, they want plenty of like, support, and encouragement. You will find a lot of things parents can do to reduce the indicators of ADHD without sacrificing the natural energy, playfulness, and sense of wonder.

1.   Take care of yourself, so you're better able to care for your kid

Eat correctly, exercise, get enough rest, find methods to lessen stress, and seek face-to-face support from family and friends as well as your child's doctor and educators.

2.   Establish structure and persist

Help your kid remain concentrated and structured

by pursuing daily routines, simplifying your child's routine, and maintaining your child occupied with healthy activities.

3.   Set obvious anticipations

Make the rules of behavior simple and clarify what will happen when they are obeyed, or broken-and continue each and every time with a motivation or an outcome.

4.   Encourage exercise and rest

Exercise enhances focus and promotes brain development. Considerably for children with ADHD, in addition, it leads to raised sleep, that may reduce the symptoms of ADHD.

5.   Help your kid eat right

To regulate symptoms of ADHD, plan regular well balanced meals or snacks every 3 hours, and cut back on junk and sweet food.

6.   Teach your kid making friends

Support him, or she becomes a far greater listener, work out how to read people's encounters and body gestures, and interact better with others.

School Approaches For Children Withith ADHD

ADHD, indeed, gets by means of learning. You can't absorb information or get work done if you're experimenting the class or zoning from what you're said to be reading or hearing. Consider what the establishing institution requires children to accomplish:

- Sit down still. Listen silently

- Give consideration. Follow instructions

- Focus

These are the items kids with ADHD have trouble doing-not because they aren't prepared, but because their brains won't let them.

However, that doesn't mean kids with ADHD can't succeed at college. You can find a lot of things both parents and instructors can do to greatly help children with ADHD thrive in the classroom. It begins with analyzing each child's specific weaknesses and advantages, then discovering creative approaches for assisting a child in focus, adhere to an activity, and work out how to utilize his/ her full capability.

Chapter 2

SYMPTOMS OF ADHD

The primary symptoms of ADHD are focusing difficulties, hyperactivity (excessive activity), and impulsivity (acting before considering the results). The behavior is normally extreme, appears before generation 7, and considerably handicaps at least two areas in someone's life (home and college, for instance).

The three main categories are:

• Inattentive: difficulty concentrating or staying devoted to a task or activity.

• Hyperactive-impulsive: extreme activity and impulsivity.

• Combined: extremely focusing on problems plus extreme activity and impulsivity.

Who is experiencing ADHD?

• 3 to 5% of children include an ADHD

- Boys are 3 x as likely as girls to become affected

- ADHD affects people of all age ranges (including adults)

Usually, it's just as time goes on; it becomes more apparent that children aren't simply daydreamers or extraordinarily active - they may be disabled having a medical disorder. For the reason that children with attention disorders show the same behaviours seen in any healthy child, except that their actions are exaggerated and debilitating. Children with ADD have a neurobiological-based impairment that triggers these to become inappropriately inattentive, and, occasionally, inappropriately impulsive with regards to generation. Many have sparse short-term remembrances, troubles in completing duties, and problems with intrusiveness.

Sleep issues will also be common. Mostly engrossed with this category are children who daydream incessantly. Because these children aren't disruptive, they could also be harder to recognize and treat. They are usually found seated in the trunk rows of classrooms, gazing out the windows. Educators may think they're "sluggish." Likely, they're not.

Those who have ADHD, rather than ADD, have the surplus challenge to become hyperactive (inappropriately active for their age). In the continuous physical whirl of unfocussed activity, they dart from here to there. Critically hampering their capacity to accomplish goals, this variant of attention disorder can wreak havoc around the family, college, and interpersonal life. ADHD (representing ADD and ADHD) impacts 2-3 times more males than women, however the teenagers who are affected could be impaired as severely as boys. It might place significant stress on parents, siblings, friends, educators, as well as others carefully linked to the kid.

Causes Of ADHD

Like all mental disorders, Attention-Deficit/Hyperactivity Disorder results from an assortment of genetic and environmental risk factors. Many studies show a little molecule in charge of communication between neurons-dopamine-plays an important role in attention, job orientation, and action. The drugs used to deal with attention-deficit/hyperactivity disorder increase its level between specific neurons. You'll be able to come with an imbalance in dopamine level. Hence, dopamine-related anxious system activities could be likely mixed up in introduction of attention-deficit/hyperactivity disorder. Since 30 to 40 percent of people who informed they have ADHD have family using the same disease, genes are often at least partially involved. Although parents, instructors, spouses, etc. usually do not cause ADHD, they are able to significantly impact the individuals capacity to handle their disorder.

Ramifications Of ADHD

A cruel consequence from the attention disorders may be the inclination towards low self-esteem. Devoid of the capability to sit down nonetheless, to attend your turn, to modify your capability to produce targets. Every one of these things makes children stand out in masses if they don't need to! Furthermore, nearly all these children have great difficulty in reading the same sociable cues that lots of children learn automatically, so they could inadvertently arrive "unusual." These children are also at higher risks for having additional mental problems such as for example stress, depression, and carry-out disorder (an inclination to become chronically disruptive, disobedient, and frequently intense).

As adults, these are in a far more significant risk for divorce, job conflict, and suicide compared to the overall population. Around 3-5% of children have ADHD, and approximately 50% of the children provides significant difficulties into adulthood. Luckily, these children could be very creative and evolve into highly accomplished adults. Perhaps, because their thoughts have a tendency to jump around a lot more than others, they have a tendency to strategize problems in unique ways. Mozart, Einstein, and Edison are suspected by many people, claiming they have an attention disorder. It's essential, aswell, to understand that this intellectual potential of the kids is not exactly like that of most of those additional general population.

You will see lawyers, doctors, school principals - people from all spheres of life - who've successfully handled their ADHD challenges. Thankfully, many of the problems with ethnic awkwardness, chronic inattentiveness, and intrusiveness often react well to guidance and group therapy. Furthermore, if these children are elevated inside a caring house and possess a knowledge college, and environment organized to meet up their needs, their probability of utilizing a positive result as adults rises significantly.

Treatments Of ADHD

Obtainable treatments are altered to meet using the needs of the average indivdual conducting a biopsychosocial assessment. Treatments include specific medications, psychoeducation, public skills training, outstanding direction at college, and specific psychotherapy.

Parents may possibly also receive help understand attention deficit disorder better and improve their parenting skills. This therapy emerges in group classes on Saturdays or at specific summer camps.

All children are also assessed to determine their response

to prescription medications in conditions of both behaviour and possible unwanted effects.

CHAPTER 3

Problems Often Connected With ADD

ADD may possibly also involve hyperactivity with behavior problems. Furthermore, students with ADD may have learning disabilities and have a tendency to maintain danger for repeated disciplinary issues in colleges. Adults and peers aswell may conclude that such students are sluggish for his or her inattention to jobs and failure to look at through with tasks. While ADD is incredibly common, misperceptions about the disorder continue steadily to circulate steadily.

How Put Differs From ADHD

Put is a term used first from the presentations of attention deficit hyperactivity disorder (ADHD), as defined in the "Diagnostic and Statistical Manual of Mental Disorders." It really is officially, "attention-deficit disorder, mainly inattentive demonstration."

ADD won't express itself just like ADHD predominantly hyperactive-impulsive type or ADHD combined kind do.

Students with these presentations have different symptoms. Children using the additional two presentations of ADHD, for instance, have a tendency to display behaviour problems consequently. Children with ADD aren't disruptive in college. They might even sit in course quietly, nonetheless it doesn't mean their disorder isn't a problem and they aren't struggling to target. Besides, not all children with ADD are aswell.

Children with ADD no hyperactivity element can happen to become bored or disinterested in classroom actions. They could be vunerable to daydreaming or forgetfulness, just work at a sluggish pace, and submit incomplete work.

Their assignment may look disorganized aswell as their desks and locker spaces. They could drop materials at college or misplace schoolwork and don't submit projects. This might frustrate educators, parents, and result in the child producing poor marks in course. Behaviour treatment may counter-attack the child's forgetfulness.

Diagnosis

In the event that you suspect your kid has ADD with or without hyperactivity, get hold of your child's college counsellor, instructor, or doctor about appropriate treatment. When you yourself have any concern, start these conversations today.

Your paediatrician may recommend seeing a youngster psychologist who are able to do formal screening on your own child to both get out if she fits certain requirements for ADD, and where she actually is actually around the spectrum. Not only can this tests help differentiate ADD from other issues that will be resulting in difficulty with assignment work, but enable you to observe a child's response to interventions as time goes on.

Treatment

ADD can also be treated with stimulant medications such as for example Ritalin. Occasionally, stimulant medications might help students with ADD stay on-task and concentrated. However, some stimulant medications have already been connected with severe part effects. As a result of this, many parents hesitate to use Ritalin, Adderall, or other drugs to deal with Increase. If parents decide to medicate their children, most doctors and child psychologists declare that a behavior involvement plan ought to be developed to greatly help train kids with adaptive behaviour skills and reduce off-task and negligent actions.

This is a lot more helpful than drug use, especially because some students informed they have ADD or ADHD don't possess these conditions but are if indeed they are doing, because of personal or family problems. Behaviour treatment programs might help students with problem behaviours if indeed they already have Add more or demonstrate ADD-like behaviours.

Indeed, there may be an advantage of long-term behaviour intervention plans, as these adaptations can lead to long-term improvement in the abilities which medication cannot provide.

Nervous About Labeling

Some parents are frightened to the fact that if indeed they have their youngster tested for ADD, she'll be labelled. Like a father or mother, however, you are able to do a great deal to prevent this from occurring. It is advisable to get hold of your child in order that she realizes that she actually is not doing anything incorrect in fighting ADD, but instead, it's your decision like a father or mother to greatly help her learn the talents that will aid her to understand as quickly as possible let her uniquely do.

CHAPTER 4

Attention Deficit Disorder Without Hyperactivity (ADD) In Adults

Attention, deficit hyperactivity disorder, is a common psychological disorder that's seen as a concern with attention, impulsivity, and hyperactivity. It might happen in adults. Adults who experience serious or persistent problems credited to six or higher from the symptoms and do not possess symptoms of hyperactivity or impulsivity may have ADD without hyperactivity. Although there is absolutely no fix for the disorder, maybe it's effectively treated with an assortment of medication and behavioral therapy.

What's attention deficit disorder without hyperactivity in adults?

Attention, deficit hyperactivity disorder, is a common psychological disorder that's seen as a concern with attention, impulsivity, and hyperactivity. Adults who've significant issues with inattention, but display few or no symptoms of hyperactivity, are believed to really have the most inattentive subtype of AD/HD.

Professional functions from the brain--such as verbal and nonverbal working memory, self-regulation and motivation, and planning--are thought to be impaired in adults with AD/HD. Adults who've AD/HD without hyperactivity can experience issues with keeping the interest and concentrating, using working storage, recalling, and regulating feelings. Organizing and prioritizing duties could be challenging.

The causes of attention deficit disorder without hyperactivity (AD/HD without hyperactivity) in adults?

Nobody is precisely absolutely sure what can cause AD/HD without hyperactivity; however, the problem often works in family. There is certainly hereditary and neurobiological basis for attention deficit disorder. Usually, adults using the mainly inattentive type of AD/HD first developed it during child years. However, because children with this type of AD/HD will never be hyperactive, the disorder might go unrecognized until they reach adolescence or adulthood. This is especially true for women and men with AD/HD without hyperactivity. Ladies could become even more silent and unaggressive than those that don't possess the disorder. Women often go undiagnosed until among their children is informed they have AD/HD. They could identify similarities within their behavior patterns and seek professional help.

Researchers are learning nutritional, environmental, and other factors that may tend involved with AD/HD.

Exactly what are symptoms of attention deficit disorder without hyperactivity (AD/HD without hyperactivity) in adults?

Predicated on the American Psychiatric Association's diagnostic manual, you will find nine (9) symptoms connected with inattention problems. Although everyone experiences many of these problems sometimes, individuals who have probably the most inattentive type of AD/HD show at least six from the nine symptoms and experience significant challenges within their day-by-day lives due to these. These symptoms might lead to disruptions within their college, work, family, or interpersonal activities. That is a couple of the nine symptoms from your mainly inattentive type of AD/HD:

1.   Often has difficulty sustaining attention at the work or playground.

2.   Frequently won't absorb details or makes careless mistakes at the work, school, or other tasks.

3.   Often has problems organizing tasks or activities.

4.   Is very easily distracted by outdoors stimuli.

5.   Frequently won't continue when given instructions or will not entirely work or school assignments, chores, or alternative activities.

6.   Often becomes forgetful when performing routine chores.

7.   Frequently puts off or avoids tasks that are looking sustained attention.

8.   Often loses materials while wanting to complete jobs or activities.

9.   Appears to never be heard despite the fact that spoken to directly.

Adults who experience serious or chronic problems, i.e., six or higher from the symptoms, nor have symptoms of hyperactivity or impulsivity may have AD/HD without hyperactivity. Other emotional circumstances, such as for example depressive disorder or panic, may also accompany the mostly inattentive type of AD/HD.

How Is Attention Deficit Disorder Without Hyperactivity (AD/HD without hyperactivity) In Adults Diagnosed?

There is no single medical or genetic test for the mainly inattentive type of AD/HD. A specialist mental doctor, just like a doctor or medical psychologist, must test the individual to have the ability to provide a diagnosis.

The physician or additional mental doctors will conduct a diagnostic interview to secure an in depth history of your past and current behaviour patterns. The discussion includes questions about how precisely you function in the home, college, and work. All your family members or friends may also be interviewed to verify and offer more information.

You will be asked about your family's track record and could be asked to endure a physical exam to remove medical ailments that may cause symptoms resembling those of ADHD.

You may be asked to complete a checklist with symptoms. The psychologist or doctor might use other behaviour ranking scales.

Other varieties of psychological assessments could be administered to get rid of the existence of co-existing conditions, such as for example anxiety or depression.

To be informed they have AD/HD, you need to be experiencing significant impairment in at least two significant parts of your lifestyle (for instance, work, college, or home). Major problems such as for example job reduction credited to inattention symptoms, extreme conflict in associations or divorce, financial problems triggered by poor business or failing to give expenses promptly, or being added to educational probation certainly are a few examples.

Some medical disorders, such as for example seizure disorders or thyroid problems, could cause symptoms resembling those of AD/HD. This is why a health check is vital to remove medical causes.

Management and Treatment

Although there is absolutely no cure for the disorder, maybe it's successfully treated. There are various methods for coping with adults, but generally, some combination of medication and behavioural therapy produces the very best results.

Medications-Prescription drugs that are used to treat AD/HD in children have a tendency to be effective for a few adults using the mostly inattentive type of AD/HD. However, the dose and rate of recurrence from the medications might need to exist adjusted. It's necessary to complement the needs of the average person with AD/HD using the characteristics from the drug.

The significant classes of prescription medications that are recommended for AD/HD are psychostimulants, antidepressants, and nonstimulant drugs. The drugs affect the neurotransmitters that send indicators to brain cells.

- Psychostimulants: would be the medications of preference in treating AD/HD. Both types that are mostly used are amphetamines and methylphenidate. Mixed amphetamine salts are promoted beneath the brand Adderall®. Methylphenidate occur beneath the brands Ritalin®, Concerta®, or Metadate®. Immediate release suffered release, and prolonged-release types of Adderall and Ritalin are available. The medication dosage and frequency from the medications might need to become modified to improve their effectiveness.

Using cases, if psychostimulants aren't useful or the average person includes a co-existing mental disorder, other medications may be recommended.

- Nonstimulants: These medications could be needed in which a patient won't respond to stimulants or posseses an adverse a reaction to them. They may be utilized for folks with co-existing psychiatric circumstances. Atomoxetine (Strattera®) was the 1st non-stimulant medication approved by the U.S. Food and Medication Administration to deal with AD/HD in adults.

• Antidepressants: Drugs such as for example tricyclic antidepressants, monoamine oxidase inhibitors, bupropion (Wellbutrin®) and venlafaxine (Effexor®) increase norepinephrine levels at heart and have a good influence around the symptoms of ADHD. These drugs aren't approved by the FDA as a result of this indicator, although they are used off-label.

Behavioural changes or various other types of therapy

Various techniques let you treat adults with inattentive problems. Therapy helps patients to identify a problem in behaviours, create, and apply, approaches for changing their behaviour and attaining goals. Behavioural changes certainly are a common approach directed at improving behaviour patterns by reinforcing desired behaviours through rewards or bonuses. Cognitive behaviour therapy targets the patient's current behaviour patterns, unlike traditional psychoanalytic therapy. It really is targeted at determining automated or irrational thoughts that can lead to negative behaviour and changing them with positive thoughts and actions. Programs have already been developed to boost self-management, however they aren't yet accessible. Group therapy may succeed for adults with AD/HD, designed for women.

Chapter 5

What Are The Differences Between ADHD and ADD? (Sign Comparison)

Attention Deficit Hyperactivity Disorder (ADHD) is a neurological or psychological disorder. Common ADHD symptoms include inattention, impulsivity, and hyperactivity in both children and adults.

The term "ADD" is often utilized to explain what clinicians now identify as Predominantly Inattentive Type ADHD. This quieter display of Attention Deficit Disorder - not connected with hyperactivity - is usually more frequent among ladies and women. Common symptoms of "ADD" include:

- Poor working memory

- Inattention

- Distractibility

- Poor professional function

The term ADHD is often utilized to explain what doctors now diagnose as Predominantly Hyperactive Type ADHD. The symptoms connected with this diagnosis align more carefully using the stereotypical understanding of ADHD:

• A squirmy, impulsive person (usually a youngster), bursting with energy

• Who struggles to attend his or her turn

Adults with hyperactive or impulsive ADHD could be:

• A talkative

• fidgety

• possess anxious energy

Theoretically speaking, Attention Deficit Disorder (ADD) is forget about a medical diagnosis. Since 1994, doctors have already been using the term "ADHD" to spell it out both hyperactive and inattentive subtypes of attention deficit hyperactivity disorder. Still, many parents, educators, and adults continue to utilize the word "ADD" when discussing inattentive symptoms and presentations from the problem.

What Exactly Are The Three Types Of ADHD?

•   Symptoms of Inattentive ADHD

People who describe themselves as having ADD probably have inattentive type ADHD. Symptoms include forgetfulness and poor concentration, organization, and hearing skills. Inattentive ADHD often resembles a sense disorder in adults, while it's considered spacey, apathetic behavior in children, especially girls.

Predicated on the Diagnostic and Statistical Manual of Mental Disorders-V (DSM-V)2, six of the next symptoms should be there to warrant a diagnosis of ADHD, Primarily Inattentive Type:

•   Often will not give close concentrate on details, or makes careless mistakes.

•   Often offers difficulty sustaining attention.

- Often won't seem to give consideration when spoken to.

- Often won't keep on instructions and will not finish projects.

- Often have a problem organizing duties and activities.

- Often avoids, dislikes, or is hesitant to tasks that want continual mental attempt.

- Often loses things needed for tasks/activities.

- Is usually often easily distracted.

- Is definitely often forgetful in way of life

If you were to think you have Primarily Inattentive Type ADHD, take our self-test and discuss your results with physician.

- Symptoms of Hyperactive-Impulsive ADHD

This sub-type has a large amount of ADHD's

stereotypical traits: a youngster (usually a boy) bouncing from your walls, interrupting in class, and fidgeting more often than not. The simple truth is, a little a part of children and adults meet the symptom criteria as a result of this sort of ADHD.

Predicated on the DSM-V, six of the next symptoms should be there to warrant a diagnosis:

• Fidgets with hands or ft. or squirms in seat.

• Leaves chair in class or in other situations where remaining seated is expected.

• Walks and works about or climb excessively in situations where maybe it's inappropriate; emotions of restlessness in teenagers and adults.

• Offers difficulty performing or taking part in leisure activities quietly.

• Appears "away from home" or functions as if "driven having a motor."

• Discussions excessively.

- Blurts out answers.

- Provides difficulty getting excited about their turn.

- Interrupts or intrudes on others

Symptoms of Combined Type ADHD occur when you have six or higher symptoms each of inattentive and hyperactive-impulsive ADHD.

What Makes Hyperactive-Impulsive ADHD Appear Different From Inattentive ADHD In Living?

1. Inattentive ADHD Indicator: Careless Mistakes

A youngster with inattentive ADHD may hurry through a quiz, missing questions he understands the answers to or skipping whole areas in his haste. A grown-up may don't carefully proofread an archive or email at the work leading to even more problems.

2. Inattentive ADHD Sign: Difficulty Sustaining Attention

A youngster with inattentive ADHD may have trouble staying concentrated during organized activities, like athletics and video gaming, or jobs. A grown-up may battle to keep up attention during extended readings or expanded conversations.

3. Inattentive ADHD Indicator: Failure to give consideration

Children and adults with inattentive ADHD can happen absent-minded when spoken to directly, despite the fact that there could not be an apparent distraction. Often won't keep on instructions and will not finish schoolwork, tasks, or responsibilities at the job (e.g., begins duties but promptly loses concentration which is easily sidetracked).

4. Inattentive ADHD Sign: Difficulty with Instructions

Many children and adults with inattentive ADHD usually keep on instructions, failing to finish schoolwork, chores, or additional duties at the job.

5. Inattentive ADHD Indicator: (Poor Organization)

An organization can be viewed as a problem for folks which have inattentive ADHD at any generation - a youngster may have a problem with keeping her locker organized; an adolescent may find it challenging to keep university applications directly, and ADHD adults might feel overwhelmed by work electronic mails at work. Inadequate organization often should go as well as messy work, poor time management, and failing woefully to meet deadlines.

6. Inattentive ADHD Sign: Avoidance of Difficult Tasks

Children and adults with inattentive ADHD frequently have trouble completing projects that are looking sustained mental work, like lengthy research tasks, reviewing documents, and completing forms.

7. Inattentive ADHD Indicator: Chronically Dropping Things

Frequently misplacing essential items, like keys, eyeglasses, cell phones, and school materials, can be viewed as an indicator of inattentive ADHD in kids, adolescents, and adults.

8. Inattentive ADHD Sign: Easily Distracted

Children with inattentive ADHD could become distracted in the classroom by extraneous stimuli, while adults may drift off into unrelated thoughts and lose focus on the duty ahead.

9. Inattentive ADHD Indicator: Forgetfulness

Whether it's remember to consider the garbage out, pay expenses, or return a contact, inattentive ADHD often presents as forgetfulness, especially in teenagers and adults.

How Is ADHD Diagnosed?

If you were to think you have among the previously listed three types of ADHD, you should go to a medical expert for the state diagnosis. You will discover more information within our comprehensive analysis guide.

Why Do More Women Have Inattentive Type ADHD Than Hyperactive-Impulsive ADHD?

ADHD isn't gender-biased, nonetheless it often moves undiagnosed in women. More women and teenagers own Inattentive ADHD than Hyperactive-Impulsive ADHD. Girls and women who've a problem with inattentive

ADHD symptoms are overshadowed by hyperactive kids, who demonstrate more stereotypical hyperactive ADHD behaviour. Instead of detecting their signs as ADHD, doctors frequently mistake them for feeling disorders.

Chapter 6

How Is ADHD Diagnosed?

Though your kid may exhibit some symptoms that look like ADHD, maybe it's another thing. That is why you'll need a physician to check on it out.

There is absolutely no specific or definitive test for ADHD. Instead, diagnosing can be an activity that will require several actions and requires gathering significant amounts of info from multiple resources. You, your kid, your son or daughter's college, and other caregivers ought to be involved in assessing your kid's behaviour. Physician may also ask what symptoms your kid has, how in the past when those symptoms began, and what sort of behaviour impacts your kid and others of all your family members. Doctors diagnose ADHD in children after a youngster shows six or higher specific symptoms of inattention or hyperactivity frequently to obtain additional than half a year in at least two configurations. The physician will think about what type of child's behaviour compares with this of additional children in the same generation. The physician gives your kid a physical exam, includes a health background, and could actually give him a noninvasive brain scan.

Your kid's primary care doctor can determine whether your kid has ADHD using standard guidelines made by the American Academy Of Pediatrics, which says the problem could be diagnosed in children ages 4 to 18. Symptoms, though, must begin by generation 12.

It's challenging to diagnose ADHD in children younger than 5. That's because many preschool children exhibit a number of the symptoms seen in ADHD in a number of situations. Also, children change rapidly through the preschool years.

Occasionally, behaviour that appears to be ADHD may be triggered instead by:

•   An abrupt life change (such as for example divorce, a death in the family, or moving out)

•   Undetected seizures

•   Medical disorders affecting brain function

- Anxiety

- Depression

- Bipolar disorder.

THREE Types Of ADHD In Children

Doctors may classify symptoms as another types of ADHD:

- Hyperactive/impulsive nature: Children show both hyperactive and impulsive behaviour, also for probably the most part, they could give consideration.

- Inattentive type: Previously called Attention Deficit Disorder (ADD). These children aren't overly active. They don't really disrupt the class or alternative activities, so their symptoms are most likely not observed.

- Mixed type (inattentive and hyperactive/impulsive): Children with this sort of ADHD display both types of symptoms. This is the most typical type of ADHD.

Drugs for Child many years of ADHD

A class of drugs called psychostimulants (or sometimes

just stimulants) is an effective treatment for child years ADHD. These medications, including Adderall, Adzenys XR-ODT, Vyvanse, Concerta, Focalin, Daytrana, Ritalin, and Quillivant XR, help children concentrate their thoughts and disregard distractions.

Another treatment used to deal with ADHD in kids is non-stimulant medication. These medications include Intuniv, Kapvay, and Strattera.

ADHD medicines comes in short-acting (immediate-release), intermediate-acting, and long-acting forms. It could take some time for physician to provide the very best medication, dose, and timetable for someone with ADHD. ADHD drugs sometimes have specific results, but these have a tendency to happen early in treatment. Usually, part effects are moderate and don't last long.

Behavioural Treatments For Children With ADHD

Behavioural treatment for children with ADHD includes creating even more structures, motivating routines, and stating expectations of a child. Other styles of ADHD treatment that may benefit your kid include:

Sociable skills training: It will help a youngster with ADHD to understand behaviours that will assist them develop and maintain social relationships.

Organizations and parenting skills training: This includes support for the parents and assisting them to find out more about ADHD as well as how exactly to father or mother a child which has ADHD.

Chapter 7

What Is A Multimodal Method Of Treating ADHD?

Multimodal treatment involves multiple means of treatment that interact to greatly help a youngster with ADHD.

The main the various parts of this technique are medications, behavioural therapy, and education.

Medications and ADHD

The recommended medicines for ADHD are stimulants. These include:

•   Amphetamine (Adzenys XR-ODT)

•   Amphetamine/Dextroamphetamine   (Adderall, Adderall XR)

•   Dexmethylphenidate (Focalin, Focalin XR)

•   Dextroamphetamine (Dexedrine or Dextrostat)

- Lisdexamfetamine (Vyvanse)

- Methylphenidate (Concerta, Daytrana, Metadate, Methylin, Quillivant XR, Ritalin)

Many of these drugs could be available in longer-acting formulations.

Non-stimulant medications used to deal with ADHD, include:

- Atomoxetine (Strattera)

- Clonidine ER (Kapvay)

- Guanfacine ER (Intuniv)

ADHD medications are used to improve children's capacity to focus and work. Sometimes, physician must prescribe different drugs or different dosages before seeking the best treatment for a youngster. Doctors and parents have to monitor children taking medications for ADHD carefully.

Unwanted side effects of ADHD medicines range between:

- Anxiety

- Reduced appetite

- Fatigue

- Irritability

- Sleeping difficulties

- Skin staining (with patches)

- Upset stomach

Most unwanted effects are small and improve after a while. Occasionally, doctors may lower a medication dosage to ease side effects.

The FDA recommends an intensive track record and exam, including an assessment of underlying center or psychiatric problems, be performed in an ADHD treatment plan. A higher risk of strokes, center attacks, and unexpected lack of life among patients with existing center conditions continues to be from the usage of ADHD medications. An increased risk of psychiatric problems, besides, continues to be connected with ADHD medications.

Behavioural Therapy And ADHD

Behavioural therapy was made to help a youngster curb challenging behaviours. This may involve helping a child work out how to organize period and actions. Alternatively, it could support complete kid homework. It might likewise incorporate assisting a child in controlling his or her impulses and reactions to psychological stimuli.

Education And ADHD

Educating parents about the disorder and its own management is usually another important a part of ADHD treatment. For parents, this may consist of learning parenting skills to greatly help a child manage his or her behavior. This may involve skills such as for example giving positive feedback for desirable behaviours, ignoring undesirable behaviours, and giving time-outs when the child's behavior has gone uncontrollable. Occasionally, the child's entire family could be involved in this section of the treatment.

ADVANTAGES OF MULTIMODAL TREATMENT

Treatment guidelines demand behaviour therapy as the utmost well-liked treatment for preschool children with ADHD. Medication could be recommended if further treatment is essential. For teenagers with ADHD, generation 6 and older, a strategy which include both behavior therapy and vaccination is preferred.

Researchers can see that multimodal treatment was particularly helpful for enhancing sociable skills in children with highly stressful conditions. Besides, it had been adequate for folks which have anxiety and major depression furthermore to ADHD.

Children who receive multimodal treatments may need lower dosages of medications compared to children only getting medication.

INDIVIDUALIZED TREATMENT PLAN

A multimodal plan is effective for a few children. This therapy and medication, however, changes regarding the specific child. Doctors, parents, and instructors have to interact to develop and administer the very best treatment for each and every child and family.

Chapter 8

ADHD Drugs: How To Handle Side Effects In Kids

The correct medicine might help kids with ADHD (Attention Deficit Hyperactivity Disorder) focus so they can finish homework and other jobs. Besides, it can benefit them fidget less and possess better social skills.

However, ADHD drugs likewise have unwanted effects which may be hard on kids -- and their parents. It often takes some learning from your own errors to obtain the proper medication and the correct dosage for your kid. Moreover, while you find the proper mixture, there could be some unwanted effects.

Monitor what sort of medication affects your kid, so you can tell the physician. If they're resulting in severe problems, a fresh medicine or different dosage could be attempted.

These pointers might help you both deal with some of the most typical unwanted effects.

1.   Insufficient Appetite

Children need a healthy, balanced diet to grow and develop precisely how they need to. When ADHD drugs get them to less starving, they could not get enough consumption of calories, nutritional vitamin supplements, and additional nourishment. Some things you can attempt:

•   Give her healthy breakfasts and dinners. When children aren't starving at lunch, they could neglect it, or they could easily get among these light snack (crackers, cheese stick, and fruit), making morning and evening meals extra important.

•   Get among these shorter-acting medications. Long-acting drugs, sometimes called prolonged release, can last the whole day. Shorter-acting drugs can wear off in 3 to 4 hours -- just as time passes for meals.

•   Have got a mini-break from medication. Ask a medical doctor if your kid can lose medication for brief intervals, like on weekends, college vacations, and breaks or before special-occasion meals.

•   When possible, give medication with breakfast

time, not before.

- Allow a bedtime treat, making up for the skipped lunchtime.

2.   Rest Problems

ADHD drugs could keep kids up at night time. That you can do if certainly they took the final dosage of your entire day too near bedtime. Alternatively, perhaps a long-acting medication hasn't worn off by night. Nevertheless, you may wait a week or two before inviting your child's doctor in the event you produce any changes towards the drug. In the interim, make sure that your child isn't taking the evening dose too close to bedtime, and make sure that your child has some activities after school to remove all of the wiggles and vigour. Sleep issues due to ADHD medicine have a tendency to get better after a while.

Moreover, take into account that overstimulation -- not medicine -- could be the reason for your child's rest issues. It could be beneficial to maintain him off gambling and his telephone or computer before bedtime.

You might try these various other tips, too:

• Make the region sleep-friendly. Light tells your body it's time and energy to exist up, so a dark room is vital. Take up a chiller if it's warm, or grab a supplementary blanket if it's cold.

• Commit to a soothing bedtime program. A nightly shower, 20 minutes of reading, or writing inside a journal might help kids unwind and drift off.

• No pets around the bed. Animals that rest on the building blocks may stretch, change positions, or maneuver around and wake your kid up.

• Countdown to rest. Tell your kid to test this mind-calming exercise: Start at 100 and count number back to 1.

OTHER COMMON UNWANTED EFFECTS

Several other possible effects include:

•   Nausea and headaches: ADHD drugs could make your kid feel like she must definitely provide. This side-effect usually goes away completely after a week or two. For the moment, your kid might look better if she'll consider her medication with food.

•   Delayed growth: Some research demonstrates that some children may grow more slowly than they have to throughout their 1st year on ADHD medicine. However, they may actually catch up during years 2 and 3. Kids, who take breaks from ADHD drugs, like on weekends and during summer vacation, might possibly not have this problem.

•   Sudden disposition changes: Some children with ADHD get cranky when their drugs wear off. That's sometimes referred to as the rebound impact. It might mean the dosage is an excessive amount of or the medication isn't befitting your son or daughter. This may also be related to never having methods to expend their vigour. Exercise might help with feel regulation.

Can You Really Treat ADHD Without Drugs?

For a few families, this implies the beginning of a protracted trek through the world of pharmaceuticals. Medications would be the top treatment for ADHD, and they're helpful for 80% of kids using the disorder.

However, many parents are worried about unwanted effects and need to exhaust another option before they put the youngster on medicine.

No real matter what your decision is, you might help your kid live a calmer, more productive life.

To Medicate Or To Never Medicate?

For some, like Joy, it had been a matter old. "My child was just five years of age when he was informed they have ADHD, and I thought that was too young for medication," she says. The American Academy of Pediatrics agrees. They generally advise that, before generation 6, you concentrate on behaviour therapy.

"Parents often ask if indeed, they are able to try additional treatments first before they consider medication, and there have been several strategies that worked," says Richard Gallagher, Ph.D., from the Institute for Attention Deficit Hyperactivity and Behaviour Disorders in the NYU Child Study Center. He encourages parents to try alternative activities while they browse the risks and benefits of medications.

Gallagher says that behaviour changes alone are most dependable with kids who are simply inattentive and unfocused, instead of those who end up also impulsive and hyperactive. Essentially the most successful treatment for ADHD combines both meds and behaviour management.

Parents And Instructors Help

Parents and classroom educators play a starring role in assisting a kid work out how to recognize and change his behaviour, Gallagher says.

For parents, therefore creating small, manageable goals for their child, such as for example seated for 10 minutes at the dining area table and giving rewards for attaining them. Additionally it is perfect for the instructor to send house a regular "record card," allowing the parents to learn if the kid met his behaviour goals at school that day.

From an age, Joy's son was graded in school every 20 minutes on three goals: staying seated, staying on task, and being respectful to others. His incentive for reaching the goals was more time capturing hoops later in your entire day - an even more effective strategy than punishing him for misbehaving, his mom says.

A trainer or tutor can work with teenagers to produce something for monitoring their books, documents, and projects, says Edward Hallowell, MD, the author of

Delivered from Distraction. "That's even more helpful than Mom or Dad attempting to support organize because, having a parent, it'll run into as nagging," he says.

Sleep

Obtaining enough shut-eye can be viewed as a game-changer for kids with ADHD. Research means that just yet another half-hour of rest might help with restlessness and impulsivity. "A lot of kids with ADHD likewise possess sleep issues, and each condition makes the other one worse," says Tag Stein, Ph.D., an ADHD specialist on the Seattle Children's Infirmary.

Probably one of the most typical rest issues for kids with ADHD is that they can not relax and drift off; then their exhaustion the following day makes their symptoms worse. Even though some doctors recommend sleep aids such as for example melatonin, you must start by practicing good sleep habits:

•   Have a continuing bedtime, even within the weekend.

- Keep the bed room cool and dark.

- Create a relaxing winding-down ritual.

"We've bedtime split into ten specific duties, like taking a bath, getting pajamas, reading for any half-hour," Pleasure says. "He previously troubles drifting off to sleep before; however, the standard support him relax."

That does mean no displays of any sort before bedtime. Take personal computers, Televisions, phones, and gambling from the bed room, meaning your son or daughter isn't sidetracked or enticed.

Exercise

Make sure that your child has a lot of opportunities to execute and fun (at appropriate times). Some recent studies found that after about 30 mins of exercise, kids with ADHD could concentrate and organize their thoughts far better.

Elise can confirm these results. "Exactly like many kids with ADHD, my child doesn't have superb coordination, but he's fallen fond of swimming," she says. "He likes the feel of water and always feels calmer when he enters the pool."

If your kid wants to try organized sports that require focus and concentration, like baseball or tennis, there's even more towards the equation. "Before they start medication, many my patients were trapped playing in the outfield, where they could simply wander around running after daisies," Stein says. "However, the medication helped them play better and be better selections from the team."

Yoga And Mindfulness

A new kind of research is exploring how mindfulness -- learning how exactly to sharpen concentration, increase awareness, and practice self-control through breathing and meditation -- might help manage the symptoms of ADHD. One little research found that when both children and their parents completed an 8-week mindfulness-training program, the children had fewer symptoms. Moreover, their parents felt less of any risk of strain that typically includes their role.

That's promising news, but Gallagher highlights that there surely is not yet enough substantial evidence to recommend the strategy. Elise's boy has attempted several different yoga techniques over time to modify his anxiousness and impulsivity. While they were helpful at the moment, she says he had not been able to adhere to them.

Music Therapy

It might hone attention and strengthen public skills. It's rhythmic and organized. Moreover, playing music requires various regions of the mind to interact, as well as learning how exactly to be always an integral part of an organization.

There's almost no hard research correctly connecting music with ADHD symptoms, but researchers can say for certain that whenever children play a drum -- taking piano lessons in the home, say, or playing cello using a school orchestra -- they may be doing much better on tests of executive function than children who don't study music. This is the ability of your brain to set up and very easily switch between tasks.

If your kid would like to kick a soccer ball instead of grab a flute, or can't sit nonetheless for lessons or practice, merely hearing her favourite playlist may relax her down long enough to complete her homework. When you focus on the music you like, the human brain produces dopamine, a substance that also supports focus. More work should be done allowing you to connect ADHD to music, but it's certainly a spot worth exploring, designed for music-loving families.

Omega-3 GAS

Over time, many "ADHD diets" have already been proposed and dismissed by science. New research factors to a connection between omega-3s and ADHD. This nourishment is situated in types of seafood such as for example salmon, in walnuts, flaxseeds, and soy products, in leafy greens, and other foods. They're also obtainable in over-the-counter supplements, aswell much like the prescription Vayarin. A report found that kids with ADHD have lower examples of omega-3s within their bloodstream, which implies bumping up the quantity within their diet might reduce ADHD symptoms.

Although omega-3 supplements aren't widely recommended as a remedy, Hallowell highlights that eating a well-balanced diet -- including fish, wholegrains, and a lot of vegetables & fruits -- and reducing sugar and processed foods will your kid live a healthy life.

Chapter 9

Parenting A Youngster With ADHD

Parents often criticize children with ADHD with regards to behavior -- but it's more good for search for and compliment good behaviour instead of punishing or holding things rear from their website for bad behaviour. Solutions to do that consist of:

• Providing obvious, constant expectations, directions, and restrictions. Children with ADHD have to discover out just what others expect from their website.

• Setting up an extremely efficient discipline system. This implies learning self-discipline methods that prize appropriate behaviour and respond to misbehaviour with alternatives such as for example periods or insufficient privileges.

• Developing a behaviour modification designed to change the most problematic behaviours. Behaviour charts that monitor your son or daughter's tasks or obligations and offering potential rewards for positive actions are proper idea tools. These charts, and various behavior adjustment techniques, might help parents address problems in organized, productive ways.

• Children with ADHD need assist in organizing their time and belongings. You are able to encourage your kid with ADHD to:

1. Adhere to a schedule: Your kid will function best if he has got the same regulars each day, from wake-up to bedtime. Be sure to consist of homework and playtime in the schedule. Kids may reap the advantages of a visual representation of their plan, just like a calendar or list. Review this with them often.

2. Organize everyday products: Your kid should have a spot for everything and keep every thing in its place. This includes clothing, backpacks, and college supplies.

3. Usage research and notebook organizers: Stress the necessity for having your kid to jot down tasks and help you with purchasing the needed books. A checklist by the finish of your day may be beneficial to make sure things like schoolbooks, lunchtime boxes, and overcoats are

brought home each day.

Methods For Doing Homework

You might help your kid with ADHD achieve academic success by taking steps to improve the grade of your kid's homework. You are able to do this by causing sure your kid is:

• Sitting within a calm area without clutter or distractions

• Encouraged to resolve each assignment inside a laptop as the teacher distributes it.

• Responsible for his/her assignments; you ought never to do for your kid what your kid can do for himself.

• Well-hydrated and given; a delicacy can do wonders for assisting to sustain attention. Try to select healthy snacks which incorporate protein. Avoid sugary meals or snacks, lacking nutrients.

Also, find out if your kid does better with a short break after school. Some kids have trouble going from college to analyze. Additional kids, though, get too sidetracked by interruptions and possess difficulty refocusing. Moreover, make sure that your child gets much exercise. Sometimes slightly added activity can do miracles for focus.

ADHD And Driving

Travelling poses special hazards for teens with ADHD. Another behaviours connected with ADHD impose serious travelling risks:

- Inattention

- Impulsivity

- Risk-taking

- Immature judgment

- Dependence on stimulation

Discuss travelling privileges together with your child based on the entire ADHD treatment plan. It really is your responsibility to determine rules and objectives for safe generating behaviours. Be sure to add a conversation about the potential risks of texting and speaking on calling while driving.

Kids With ADHD And Relationships

Not all children with ADHD have trouble getting along with others. If your kid will, however, you might take the appropriate steps to aid in improving his or her ethnic skills and human relationships. The earlier your child's issues with peers are resolved, the more profitable such measures could be. It really is perfect for you to:

• Recognize the necessity for healthy peer relationships for children.

• Involve your kid in activities together with his or her peers; choosing an activity your child is usually exceptionally effective in or loves might help them to really have the self-confidence had a need to focus on interesting more with peers.

• Place up friendly behaviour goals together with your child and implement a motivation program.

• Encourage public interactions if your kid is usually withdrawn or excessively shy.

• Routine play actions with only 1 other child at exactly the same time.

• Supervise play actions as your kid practices interpersonal skills. If something doesn't go well, process it with her later. Maybe try role-playing to find out what she could own said or done differently.

ADHD Diet And Nutrition

Can everything you take in support attention, focus, or hyperactivity? There is absolutely no very clear scientific evidence that ADHD is due to diet or nutritional problems. However, particular foodstuffs may fun at least some role in affecting symptoms in just a little group, research suggests.

So are there certain things you must not eat when you have the problem? Listed here are answers to questions about elimination diets, supplements, and foods that may ease symptoms from the disorder.

What's An ADHD Diet?

They might be the foodstuffs you ingest and any supplements you may take. Preferably, your daily diet plans should help your brain better and reduce symptoms, such as for example restlessness or insufficient focus. You could focus on these choices:

• Overall nutrition: The assumption is that some foods you ingest will make your symptoms better or worse. You might not be eating some things that might help get symptoms better.

• Supplementation diet: With this program of action, you add nutritional vitamin supplements, nutrients, or other diet. The theory is definitely that it could help you create up for not getting enough from the through everything you ingest. Supporters from the diets think that in the event that you don't acquire enough of precise nourishment, it could support and boost your symptoms.

• Removal diets: These involve not attempting to

consume foods or things that you imagine may be triggering sure habits or making your symptoms worse.

Eat Nutritious Food

ADHD diets haven't been researched a good deal. Data is bound, and email details are combined. Many health experts, though, think that what you ingest and drink might help ease symptoms.

Experts say that whatever is lovely for the mind might be best for ADHD. You may eat:

• A high-protein diet: Coffees, cheese, eggs, meat, and crazy can be exceptional sources of protein. Eat these kinds of foods every day as well for after-school snacks. It might improve concentration as well as perhaps help to make ADHD medications work a lot longer.

• Even more complex sugars: They are the nice guys. Bunch on vegetables and several fruits, including oranges, tangerines, pears, grapefruit, apples, and kiwi. Eat this sort of food during the night, and it might assist you to rest.

• Even more omega-3 efa's: You will discover these in tuna, salmon, and other cold-water white fish. Walnuts, Brazil nuts, olive and canola oils are other foods with these in them. You may have an omega-3 oily acid supplement. The FDA approved an omega compound called Vayarin in an ADHD management strategy.

Foods To Try Manage ADHD

Decrease on what several you ingest the next Simple carbohydrates:

• Candy

• Corn syrup

• Honey

• Sugar

• Products produced from white flour

• White rice

• Potatoes without skins.

SUPPLEMENTS FOR ADHD

Some experts advise that people with ADHD experience a 100% vitamin and nutrient supplement each day. Various other diet experts, though, believe that individuals who take in a typical, well-balanced diet don't need a supplement or micronutrient supplements. They say there is absolutely no scientific evidence that vitamin or mineral supplements help all children who've got the disorder. While a multivitamin could be okay when children, teens, and adults don't eat balanced diets, mega-doses of vitamins could be toxic. Prevent them.

ADHD symptoms differ from person to person. Work with a medical doctor closely if you're considering taking a supplement. To look at among these, you select a particular food or element you think may be producing your symptoms worse. Afterward you don't eat anything with this in it. If the symptoms progress or disappear entirely, you then retain steering clear of that food.

In the event that you slice some of food from your own daily diet, achieved it improve your symptoms? Research in these areas is ongoing, and the e-mail address details aren't clear-cut. Most researchers don't recommend this technique for controlling ADHD, however, still, here are some common parts of concern and what professionals suggest:

- Food additives:

In 1975, an allergist initial proposed that artificial colours, flavours, and preservatives might trigger hyperactivity in a few children. After that, experts and child behaviour experts have hotly debated this matter.

Some said the very thought of cutting those ideas from the diet is unfounded and unsupported by technology. However, one research demonstrates some food colour and one preservative do make some children more hyperactive. However, the consequences varied associated with generation and additive.

Based on this and various other recent studies, the American Academy of Pediatrics now agrees that removing preservatives and food colourings from this diet can be an acceptable option for children with ADHD.

Some experts advise that people with ADHD prevent these chemicals:

• Artificial Colours, especially red and yellow

Some studies have linked hyperactivity towards the preservative sodium benzoate, and food additives such as for example aspartame, MSG (monosodium glutamate), and nitrites.

• Sugars: Some children become hyperactive after eating chocolate or other sugary foods. No proof implies that this is grounds behind ADHD, however, for the best overall nourishment, sugary foods ought to be a little a part of anyone's diet. Nevertheless, you can test trimming them to learn if symptoms improve.

Caffeine: Small amounts of it might help with some ADHD symptoms in children, studies also show. However, the aspect effects of caffeine may outweigh any potential advantage. Most experts advise that individuals eat or drink less caffeine or avoid it. Invest the medication for ADHD, caffeine could make some unwanted effects worse.

Chapter 10

Caffeine And ADHD

The most typical treatment for ADHD is stimulant therapy. These drugs can improve your concentrate and attention period and help control impulsive behavior. The latest stimulant, and the most used medication in the world, is caffeine. It's in espresso, tea, chocolate, soda, and other foods.

Many studies have viewed how caffeine erupts difference ADHD symptoms; however, the results have already been combined. Although caffeine is a stimulant, it is not generally suggested as an end to ADHD because it hasn't become as efficient as prescription drugs.

How It Operates

Stimulants, including caffeine, enhance the quantity of specific chemicals that this mind uses to send indicators. Among these is dopamine. It's connected with pleasure, attention, and motion.

When you yourself have ADHD, doctors often prescribe

stimulants to assist you look calmer and focused. Some experts believe that because studies show the caffeine in tea can improve alertness and focus, it might work for ADHD, too.

Some scientists think caffeine has potentials as an ADHD treatment because of its influence on dopamine levels, which improves storage and attention in rats. In another research, when hyperactive rats received caffeine before they experienced a maze, they advanced at it. This suggests caffeine can improve spatial learning. While these studies are interesting, rats aren't people.

The Downside

Greater than 400 milligrams of caffeine is a lot much more likely to cause problems including:

- Migraine headaches

- Insomnia

- Irritability

- Upset stomach

A study found that caffeine was considerably less effective than dextroamphetamine (Dexedrine) and methylphenidate (Concerta, Ritalin), two types of medication popular to deal with ADHD.

For Children

Experts don't recommend offering caffeine to children, especially if they're taking prescription medications for ADHD. Kids could become more susceptible to the medial side effects of caffeine. Moreover, it could produce a different brain development in growing children.

While an adult study found that high doses of caffeine (600 milligrams) each day helped control hyperactivity symptoms in children, there were many side results.

Kids with ADHD generally have more sleep problems and possess trouble staying alert during the day. Caffeine can disrupt rest, which can make these issues worse.

The American Academy of Pediatrics recommends that no children will need to have energy drinks, as the high examples of stimulants -- including caffeine -- could cause serious medical issues.

Adult ADHD And Exercise

ADHD doesn't just affect children. Adults can possess this issue, too. ADHD helps it be hard for adults to provide consideration, control their feelings, and finish jobs.

Precisely like kids, adults with ADHD have a tendency to get stimulants or additional medications to modify symptoms. They could likewise have therapy classes to greatly help obtain structured and stay concentrated.

Research is discovering that getting regular fitness can improve considering ability, and it might improve the symptoms of adult ADHD.

Exercise Your Brain

The practice isn't just best for shedding surplus fat and toning muscles. It can benefit keep carefully the brain in better form, too. When you exercise, the mind produces chemicals called neurotransmitters, including dopamine, that help with attention and clear thinking. Individuals who have ADHD frequently have less dopamine than typical within their mind.

The stimulant medicines you can use to take care of adult ADHD work is by increasing the choice of dopamine at heart. So it is usually practically a good work out that can own many of the same results as stimulant drugs. Fitness can experience the next benefits for adults with ADHD:

• Ease anxiety and stress

• Improve impulse control and reduce compulsive behaviour

• Enhance working storage

• Improve professional function, i.e., the band of skills needed to plan, organize please remember exact details

• Increase levels of brain-derived neurotrophic factor. That is clearly a protein associated with learning and storage. It's a concern in individuals who have ADHD.

More Factors To Exercise

Beyond supporting with ADHD symptoms, exercise has other benefits. Getting regular activities can help you:

• Stay at a healthy weight. That's important because proof shows that people with ADHD can be obese.

• Reduce your risk of coronary disease, diabetes, and sure types of cancer.

• Keep your blood pressure and cholesterol levels in a typical range.

• Strengthen your bone tissue.

• Improve your mood and self-esteem.

How Often Do You Exercise?

Health experts advise that you reach least 150 minutes of average intensity exercise weekly. That computes to about 30 mins of fitness every day, five occasions a week.

If you're doing more extreme aerobic exercise routines -- such as for example working or taking indoor bicycling classes -- you are able to escape with about 75 minutes of exercise weekly. Whatever sort of exercise you must do. For example, you can attempt operating, biking, taking an aerobics course, or weight training exercise. Do whatever sort of workout you prefer.

Try to vary your exercise routine. That way, you won't weary or concentrate halfway through your exercises. You can even change activities mid-routine, for instance, by doing interval training. Run or routine for 30 a few moments, alternated with 30 secs to 1 minute of weight lifting.

CHAPTER 11

Meditation And Yoga Exercise For ADHD

Medication and therapy are good methods to control ADHD symptoms. However, they're not your only options. Research now demonstrates mindfulness yoga -- where you positively notice your moment-to-moment thoughts and emotions- -- may also be a sensible way to relax the human brain and improve your concentration. More excellent when compared to a third of adults with ADHD use this practice, and about 40% give it high rankings, according to a 2017 study.

Unlike additional treatments, mindfulness meditation doesn't need a prescription or a vacation to a therapist's office. You are able to practice it seated or walking, and even through some types of pilates.

How It Operates

Every time a specific muscle is weak, you are able to do exercises to create it stronger. The same thing holds for the mind. Mindfulness, yoga breathing strengthens your capacity to regulate your attention. It explains how exactly to see yourself and to focus on something. Moreover, it trains you to create your wandering brain back again to once you obtain side-tracked. Additionally, it could make you be more aware of your feelings, so you're less likely to act impulsively.

Mediation is known as to aid with ADHD because it thickens your prefrontal cortex, a fundamental element of the mind that's associated with concentration, planning, and impulse control. Besides, it does increase your brain's amount of dopamine, which can be a concern in ADHD brains.

Research means that mindfulness meditation could be very helpful in relieving ADHD symptoms. One landmark UCLA research discovered that people with ADHD who visited a mindfulness yoga session once weekly for 2 and 1/2 hours, then completed a normal home yoga breathing practice that continuously increased from 5 to quarter-hour over eight weeks, were better able to stay devoted to tasks. They were also less consumed with stress and stressed. Other studies after that experienced similar results.

Yoga has shown to aid in improving ADHD symptoms, too, although a lot of the report continues to be finished with children. Like mindfulness yoga, it ups dopamine levels and strengthens the prefrontal cortex. One research found that kids who used yoga approaches for 20 minutes twice weekly for eight weeks improved on assessments that measure attention and concentration.

Other Benefits

Beyond assisting to realize their symptoms, this sort of rest technique may also help individuals who have ADHD:

- Boost self-esteem

- Lower stress

- Lose weight

Because individuals who have ADHD may have trouble getting stuff done promptly and may be forgetful, they have a tendency to be very critical of themselves. Nevertheless, you should use yoga breathing as a musical instrument to tune out the judgmental modulation of voice in your thoughts.

People who regularly do mindfulness yoga have already been found to have lower examples of stress hormones when they're in configurations or situations that cause stress, like if you are feeling helpless and uncontrollable.

Research also demonstrates that mindfulness meditation can lead to slimming down, probably because it encourages you to trust more carefully about everything you're doing, including everything you take in.

Options For Meditating With ADHD

Are so many things running through your brain? Photo a blue sky with fluffy white clouds. The sky represents your consciousness; the clouds symbolize your ideas. Focus on the days of "space" in the middle of your clouds to redirect yourself.

When you yourself have trouble staying still, moving yoga breathing as you stroll could be just as good as a seated version. Whenever the human brain wanders; softly bring your attention back to the feelings around the bottoms of the ft.

What's The Most Effective Exercise To Regulate ADHD Symptoms?

It's likely you have already heard that regular exercise can offer your mood with a good start. When you yourself have ADHD, an excellent exercise may cause you to feel great. It could be good for control your symptoms, too.

A fantastic single session of moving your body could cause you to become more motivated for mental tasks, increase your brainpower, give you vigour, and assist you to look less puzzled. It functions within the human brain generally in most from the same ways as your ADHD medication.

To reap these rewards, though, you need to exercise the way in which and at the proper amount. The real key is to discover a task that fits the right path of life and persist.

Obtain The Most Out Of Active

The results of exercise only last for so very long, precisely like medicine. Consider your workout as a remedy, "dosage." Aim for at least one 30- to 40-minute activity each day, 4 or 5 days weekly.

The exercise you decide on is your decision, but make certain it's "moderately intense," meaning during your workout:

- Your heartrate goes up

- You breathe harder and faster

- You sweat

- Muscle tissue feel tired

Get hold of your doctor if you're unsure how extreme your exercise ought to be. She may recommend you have a heartrate monitor or several other devices to be certain you acquire the most out of the workout.

Types Of Exercise You Are Able To Do

- Aerobic exercise: That's whatever gets you pounding. You must do a thing that boosts your heartrate and maintains it there for an organized timeframe, like around thirty minutes to 40 minutes.

Aerobic exercise creates fresh pathways in the mind and floods it using the chemicals that assist you to give consideration. You can attempt among the following:

- Running

- Walking briskly

- Biking

- Swimming laps

You can certainly do these activities outside or indoors, but when you have a choice, go out. Studies show that being in character when you move can lessen your ADHD symptoms a lot more than when you exercise inside.

- Fighting techniques: Experts state the greater technical your exercise is, the better for the mind. Athletics like karate, taekwondo, jiujitsu, and judo focus on self-control and combining your brain and body. When you do fighting techniques, you get been trained in skills like:

- Concentration

- Balance

- Timing

- Memory

If fighting techniques isn't your thing, alternative activities that also help the problem in human brain and body are:

- Rock climbing

- Dance

- Gymnastics.

- Yoga

- Strength training: If you're only just getting started off with exercise, choose aerobic pursuits like walking or running initially. Once you've been at it for quite a while, then add power work for variety. Try exercises like:

- Lunges

- Squats

- Pushups

- Pullups

- Weightlifting

- Team sports: In the event that you join a softball or soccer little league, it could be just essential to truly get you up and moving often weekly. Organized athletics have all of the advantages of exercise using the added reward of the interpersonal group to motivate you.

Teamwork hones your communication skills and will help you think about your actions and plan. Being area of the team may also improve your self-esteem.

How To Keep At It

The same as medicine, exercise just might help you treat ADHD in the event that you keep writing. However, in the event that you find yourself having an attention span, how do you want to keep up with the course? Try the following tips:

•   Hold it interesting: You are able to stay from the rut in the event that you change your activity each day or week.

•   Appear for somebody: An excellent workout buddy can help you stick to track and help you at that time when you sweat.

Move around each day hours: If it fits in your program, exercise ought to be the initial thing every day before you take your medication. That way, you'll have the most great things about all of the excess mood-boosting chemicals within you

Acknowledgements

The Glory of this book success goes to God Almighty and my beautiful Family, Fans, Readers & well-wishers, Customers, and Friends for their endless support and encouragement.